Judicial Independence in China: An Attainable Principle?

Erasmus University Rotterdam

Judicial Independence in China: An Attainable Principle?

Inaugural Lecture

Delivered on the occasion of accepting the position of professor of Chinese law at the Erasmus University Rotterdam on Thursday, 1 November 2012

Yuwen Li

eleven
international publishing

Published, sold and distributed by Eleven International Publishing
P.O. Box 85576
2508 CG The Hague
The Netherlands
Tel.: +31 70 33 070 33
Fax: +31 70 33 070 30
e-mail: sales@budh.nl
www.elevenpub.com

Sold and distributed in USA and Canada
International Specialized Book Services
920 NE 58th Avenue, Suite 300
Portland, OR 97213-3786, USA
Tel: 1-800-944-6190 (toll-free)
Fax: +1 503 280-8832
orders@isbs.com
www.isbs.com

Eleven International Publishing is an imprint of Boom uitgevers Den Haag.

ISBN 978-94-90947-92-7

Printed in The Netherlands

Table of Contents

1 Introduction

China has an immensely sized judicial body with the Supreme People's Court (SPC) at the central level, 32 higher people's courts at the provincial level, 409 intermediate people's courts at the city level and 3,117 basic people's courts at the county and district levels.[1] There are approximately 200,000 judges working at the various tiers of the court system. The Chinese judiciary is operating within a political system where the functions of the legislature, executive and judiciary are divided into three branches without a strong separation of powers. Contentiously, these powers are all under the unchallengeable leadership of the Communist Party. Increasingly, the Chinese judiciary is confronted with thorny disputes, ranging from compensation for laid-off workers and rural farmers to mass litigation against local government, which emerge as a consequence of the country's rapid economic and social transition. Furthermore, the Chinese judiciary is increasingly scrutinised by the social media; both freedom of expression and the right to information have occasionally exposed a pattern of courts handling cases in a hasty and seldom critical manner. Unsurprisingly, judicial independence in China has generated profound concerns among legal scholars both inside and outside of China. Aside from the soaring debate of critics within China, which unfortunately cannot be fully comprehended by foreigners due to the language barrier, there is also a rising number of English publications tackling the troublesome issue of judicial independence in China.[2]

In this inaugural lecture, I aim to examine both the advances in, and limits of, judicial independence in China from the perspective of both

1 'Renmin Fayuan Jianjie' (A brief introduction to people's courts), <www.court.gov.cn/jgsz/rmfyjj/>. Last visited September 2012.

2 See Randall Peerenboom (ed.), *Judicial Independence in China: Lessons for Global Rule of Law Promotion*, (Cambridge: Cambridge University Press, 2010). Margaret Y.K. Woo, 'Adjudication Supervision and Judicial Independence in the P.R.C.', (1991) 39 *The American Journal of Comparative Law*, pp. 95-119; Hikota Koguchi, 'Some Observations About "Judicial Independence" in Post-Mao China', in R.H. Folsom and J.H. Minan (eds.), *Law in the People's Republic of China: Commentary, Readings and Materials*, (Dordrecht: M. Nijhoff Publishers, 1989), pp. 189-197; Marie Seong-Hak Kim, 'A Distant Premise: Judicial Independence in the People's Republic of China', (1996) 24 *Korean Journal of Comparative Law*, pp. 17-42; Liao Kuangsheng, '"Independent Administration of Justice" and the PRC Legal System', (1983) XVI (2-3) *Chinese Law and Government*, pp. 123-152. Xin Ren, *Tradition of the Law and Law of the Tradition, Law, State, and Social Control in China*, (Connecticut: Greenwood Press, 1997), pp. 47-63.

the legislation and judicial practice. It is widely accepted that the gap between law in books and law in action can be huge in contemporary China.[3] This is predominantly due to the reconstruction of the country's legal system which has a short history of approximately 30 years, and as such priority has been given to law-making, which is far easier to achieve than the complex process of law enforcement. However, as legal development ensues, the implementation of law is inevitably progressing and consequently demanding more attention. The judicial system and its independence lie at the crux of formalizing and reshaping the legal landscape.

3 Donald Clark, 'Power and Politics in the Chinese Court System: the Enforcement of Civil Judgments', (1996) 10 (1) *Columbia Journal of Asian Law*. Randall Peerenboom, *China's Long March toward Rule of Law*, (Cambridge: Cambridge University Press, 2002).

2 The Notion and Implications of Judicial Independence

Nowadays, judicial independence is widely accepted as covering both the independence of judges (internal independence) and the independence of courts (institutional independence). With regard to the independence of judges, Fiss identifies three dimensions: 'party detachment', requiring judges to be free from parties involved in a case; 'individual autonomy', which refers to collegial relations with other judges as well as between judges in higher and lower courts; 'political insularity', which demands that judges act independently from political institutions and the public at large.[4] Larkins describes an independent judge as a 'neutral third' who 'can be trusted to settle controversies after considering only facts and their relations to relevant laws'.[5] He further explains that such independence requires judges to have two characteristics. One is impartiality, which can be assessed as to 'judges' attitudes and beliefs as well as their behaviour *vis-à-vis* particular political and social actors'. The other is insularity, describing how 'judges should not be used as tools to further political aims nor punished for preventing their realization'.[6] Apart from political detachment, some legal scholars also stress that judges be free from blandishment or other interference by private citizens when deciding cases.[7]

To enable judges to perform their functions independently, we also need to provide institutional protection against possible intimidations. Hence, in the words of Ferejohn, judicial independence 'is a feature of the institutional setting within which judging takes place'.[8] This is referred to by various scholars as the institutional independence of courts. It depicts how a court 'has a distinct and discrete role – detached

---

4 Owen Fiss, 'The Limits of Judicial Independence', (1993) 25 (58) *U. Miami Inter-Am. L. Rev.*, pp. 59-60. For a more shielding view on inseparability between politics and the judiciary in current China, see Zhu Suli, '"Judicial Politics" as State-Building', in Stephanie Balme and Michael W. Dowdle (eds.), *Building Constitutionalism in China*, (New York: Palgrave Macmillan, 2009), pp. 23-36.

5 Christopher M. Larkins, 'Judicial Independence and Democratization: A Theoretical and Conceptual Analysis', (1996) 44 *The American Journal of Comparative Law*, p. 608.

6 *Ibid*, p. 609.

7 Keith S. Rosenn, 'The Protection of Judicial Independence in Latin America', (1987) 19 *U. Miami Inter-Am. L. Rev.*, p. 7.

8 John Ferejohn, 'Independent Judges, Dependent Judiciary: Explaining Judicial Independence', (1999) 72 *Southern California Law Review*, p. 353.

from the interests of the political system, the concerns of powerful social groups, or the desires of the general public – to regulate the legality of state acts, enact justice, and determine general constitutional and legal values'.[9] In the context of critical assessment of judicial independence in the USA, Ferejohn points out that 'the more genuine threats to judicial independence – if we interpret it as providing a broad guarantee that people can have their disputes decided in front of independent judges – are not really the sporadic attacks on individual judges, but instead are found in attempts to diminish or regulate the powers of the judiciary as a whole'.[10]

In order to gain a more concrete understanding of the hallmarks and key implications of judicial independence, further elaboration on its internal and institutional forms is required. Here I would like to refer to the Basic Principles on the Independence of the Judiciary endorsed by the General Assembly of the United Nations in 1985, to identify the implications of judicial independence.[11] The General Assembly Resolution is a result of the United Nations efforts to codify rules of judicial independence in the 1980s.[12] It contains 20 basic principles, all of which can be classified into three core components: personal independence, institutional independence, and financial independence.[13]

9 Christopher M. Larkins, *supra* note 5, p. 611.

10 John Ferejohn, *supra* note 8, p. 360.

11 General Assembly Resolution 40/32 of 29 November 1985, UN Doc. A/RES/40/32. The document is available at <www2.ohchr.org/english/law/indjudiciary.htm>. Last visited September 2012.

12 CIJL (The Centre for the Independence of Judges and Lawyers) Bulletin 25-26, Special Issue, *The Independence of Judges and Lawyers: A Compilation of International Standards*, 1990, p. 7.

13 It should be noted that the UN Basic Principles on the Independence of the Judiciary do not specifically use the terms of 'personal', 'institutional', or 'financial' independence. Personal independence is used in the IBA Minimum Standards of Judicial Independence adopted by the International Bar Association in 1982. The two documents contain similar principles, only the IBA Standards concretize 46 standards and order them under seven clear subtitles: judges and the executive; judges and the legislature; terms and nature of judicial appointments; the press, the judiciary and the courts; standards of conduct; securing impartiality and independence; and the internal independence of the judiciary. The text of the IBA Minimum Standards of Judicial Independence is available at <www.ibanet.org/About_the_IBA/IBA_resolutions.aspx>. Last visited September 2012. The most recently updated standards on juridical independence drafted by a group of internationally known legal scholars and jurists is the 2008 Mt Scopus International Standards of Judicial Independence. The text is available at <http://law.huji.ac.il/upload/InternationalStandardsof judicialInd2008.doc>. Last visited September 2012. For a brief discussion of the Mt. Scopus Standards and the interaction between domestic law and international law concerning judicial independence, see Shimon Shetreet, 'The Normative Cycle of Shaping Judicial Independence in Domestic and International Law: The Mutual Impact of National and International Jurisprudence and Contemporary Practical and Conceptual Challenges', (2009) 10 (1) *Chicago Journal of International Law*, pp. 275-332.

Personal independence refers to the qualifications, terms of office and basic rights of judges. It provides that persons selected for a role in the judiciary should be individuals of integrity and ability, with appropriate training or qualification in law (Principle 10); 'the term of office of judges, their independence, security, adequate remuneration, conditions of service, pensions and the age of retirement shall be secured by law' (Principle 11); judges should have guaranteed tenure (Principle 12), enjoy personal immunity from civil suits for improper acts or omissions in the exercise of judicial functions (Principle 16), enjoy the freedoms of expression, belief, association and assembly provided that such rights are conducted in a manner in compliance with the dignity, impartiality and independence of the judiciary (Principle 8); and, any charge or complaint against a judge with regard to exercising his judicial function should be handled expeditiously with a fair procedure (Principle 17).

Institutional independence wrestles with a court's relationship with the government and other organs of a state. Fundamentally, the state is required to provide for the independence of the judiciary in its Constitution or other laws and obliges all governmental and other institutions to respect and observe the independence of the judiciary (Principle 1). The judiciary should decide matters before them impartially 'without any restrictions, improper influences, inducements, pressures, threats or interferences, direct or indirect, from any quarter or for any reason' (Principle 2). The judiciary should have jurisdiction over all issues with a judicial nature and have the exclusive authority to decide whether it is competent, according to law to make a decision on the issues at stake (Principle 3). There should be no inappropriate interference with the judicial process; furthermore, judicial decisions should not be revised unless by judicial review in accordance with the law (Principle 4). Judicial proceedings are to be conducted fairly by the judiciary and the rights of the parties are to be respected (Principle 6).

Financial independence requires the State to provide adequate resources to enable the judiciary to perform its functions effectively (Principle 7).

Furthermore, in 1989 the UN General Assembly endorsed the 'Procedures for the Effective Implementation of the Basic Principles on the Independence of the Judiciary' to call upon all States to adopt and implement the Basic Principles in their administration of justice.[14] Since 1994 the UN Commission on Human Rights and, subsequently, its Human Rights Council has appointed a Special Rapporteur on the independence of judges and lawyers with the mandate to inquire into any substantial allegations attacking the independence of judges and lawyers in individual States, identify problems, and make recommendations on a vast array of issues concerning enhancing judicial independence in the States concerned and in general.[15]

14 The procedures were adopted by the Economic and Social Council in Resolution 1989/60 and endorsed by the UN General Assembly in Resolution 44/162, adopted on 15 December 1989. See <www.un.org/documents/ga/res/44/a44r162.htm>. Last visited September 2012.

15 Special Rapporteur on the Independence of Judges and Lawyers, <www.ohchr.org/EN/Issues/Judiciary/Pages/IDPIndex.aspx>. Last visited September 2012.

3 The Current Status of Judicial Independence in Chinese Law

Generally speaking, under the current legal framework, China recognizes the independence of courts, but fails to fully acknowledge and appreciate the independence of judges.

The independence of courts was initially propounded in 1954 through the enactment of the first Constitution of the People's Republic of China. Article 78 stated that 'people's courts shall conduct adjudication independently and shall be subject only to the law'. However, this constitutional principle was removed in the subsequent 1975 and 1978 Constitutions. In 1982, the Constitution re-established the principle of judicial independence. Article 126 proclaims that: 'The people's courts shall, in accordance with the law, exercise judicial power independently and are not subject to interference by administrative organs, public organisations or individuals.' This provision is then repeated in Article 4 of the Organic Law of People's Courts (1983), Article 6 of the Civil Procedure Law (1991), Article 5 of the Criminal Procedure Law (1996), and Article 1 of the Judges Law (1995).

As to the exclusion of the independent administration of justice by judges, Jiang Hua, former President of the Supreme People's Court (1978-1983) once explained that the courts should comply with the principle of democratic centralism in administering justice. This means that 'aside from the minority being subject to the majority, the lower level should be subordinate to a higher level, the individual should be subordinate to the organisation, and the entire Party should be subordinate to the Central Committee. Therefore, a verdict can be valid only after its approval by the court president and presiding judge'. He further pointed out that 'the collegiate bench is a temporary set-up of the people's court to conduct trials. It cannot exercise the power of administering justice on behalf of the court. Therefore, its verdict can become effective only after the people's court has set its seal to the verdict.'[16] However, such conceptions can no longer be relied upon to rouse overwhelming support in modern-day China.

16 'A Discussion of How the People's Courts Administer Justice Independently', Zhongguo fazhi bao (Chinese Legal Daily), 29 May, 1981. Quoted from Liao Kuangsheng, *supra* note 2, p. 147.

Progress is reflected in the Judges Law promulgated in 1995, which could be portrayed as having contributed to judicial independence. Article 8 prescribes a number of rights vested in judges, including the right 'to brook no interference from administrative organs, social organisations and individuals in trying cases according to law'; the right to not be dismissed, demoted, removed or given a sanction without legal basis and following legal procedure; the right to receive remuneration, enjoy insurances and welfare benefits; the judges' personal property and residential safety are protected by law; the right to participate in training; and the right to lodge petitions or complaints. Article 45 further provides that if such non-interference is violated, the responsibility of the relevant organs and individuals for such interference should be investigated.

While recognizing the positive legal provisions relating to judicial independence, we should also examine those contentious legal provisions that may undermine judicial independence. First, the Constitution prohibits administrative organs, social organizations and individuals from interfering in court proceedings, in order to allow the courts to carry out their adjudicative powers independently. It is, however, silent about the position of the Communist Party and its organs at various levels. Moreover, the Preamble of the Constitution reinforces the leadership of the Communist Party in all State affairs, including most importantly judicial affairs. Consequently, this legitimises the Party's dominance over judicial work and has resulted in the courts being expected to serve and implement the Party's major policies alongside the reality that the Party's organs interfere with individual cases before courts.[17] Another Constitutional provision that casts some doubt on judicial independence is Article 129, which grants the People's Procuratorate the power of legal supervision, including supervision of the courts' work. This constitutional specification has been concretized, particularly in the Criminal Procedure Law.[18]

In addition, the Judges Law contains a political prerequisite as one of the qualifications for being a judge. Article 9 provides that judges must have good political, professional ethics and upright conduct. In China, good political ethics is commonly understood to mean the supporting

---

17 Xianchu Zhang, 'Civil Justice Reform with Political Agendas', in Yu Guanghua (ed.), *The Development of the Chinese Legal System: Change and Challenges*, (London and New York: Routledge, 2011), pp. 253-265.

18 See Art. 243 of the 2012 revised Criminal Procedure Law.

and pursuing of communist ideology and policy. Judges' political allegiances may prevent them from strictly following the law in adjudicating cases when a Party policy contravenes the law. Most notably, the 'strike hard against crimes' campaigns have taken place periodically since 1983 under the leadership of the Political and Legal Committee of the Party, during which time the courts, procuratorates and police cooperated closely in undermining legal procedures and imposing harsh punishments.[19]

In sum, current Chinese laws demand only a limited respect for the principle of judicial independence. While the laws recognize that courts are to perform judicial functions independently, according to law, and without interference by administrative organs, social organizations and individuals, the laws do not explicitly exclude interferences by the Communist Party, from the legislative organs, or from higher courts. The Judges Law provides judges with the right to adjudicate cases according to law without interference from administrative organs, social organizations and individuals, but the Law does not confirm a judge's independence in adjudicating cases subject to only law. Neither does it exclude interference from legislative organs, a judge's superior, or a judge's colleague. The independence of judges is highly valued in contemporary society because ultimately the final guarantee of the citizens' rights as provided for in the law is in the hands of the judges. It has been rightly suggested that law 'loses its force when a judge cannot conduct a trial independently and render an equitable verdict because of the fear of losing his or her position and facing political persecution'.[20] Consequently, Chinese laws require amendment and subsequent improvement in order to provide a clearer and broader range of judicial independence.

19 Susan Trevaskes, *Policing Serious Crime in China: From 'Strike Hard' to 'Kill Fewer'*, (London and New York: Routledge, 2010). Sarah Biddulph, *Legal Reform and Administrative Detention Powers in China*, (Cambridge: Cambridge University Press, 2007).
20 Marie Seong-Hak Kim, *supra* note 2, p. 33.

4 Judicial Independence in Practice

In this part of my lecture, I will firstly discuss the efforts that have been made in constructing an independent judiciary, and then dependence characteristics in practice.

4.1 The Impressive Efforts Towards Constructing an Independent Judiciary

Over the last thirty years of judicial construction and reform, a set of measures have been implemented, which have been conducive to strengthening judicial independence in China. A first one to mention is the introduction and implementation of the National Judicial Examination system since 2002. There was a considerable shortage of judges with formal legal education as a result of the closing of law schools for more than ten years during the Cultural Revolution. Legal education was only resumed in a few comprehensive universities in 1977 and the law graduates could not satisfy the demand for legally-trained judges during the 1980s and 1990s. As a result, thousands of demobilized military officers were recruited into courts. Parallel to the resumption and expansion of normal legal education at universities, in March 2002, the first National Judicial Examination was held. Since then most of the newly-recruited judges have passed the examination which has gradually made the composition of judges with formal legal education the majority in courts. However, courts in remote areas continue to face a lack of professionally trained judges. A proper legal education for judges is required by the nature of judicial work. Judicial independence can only be expected to be vested in those who possess legal knowledge and skills in adjudicating cases according to law.

A second measure worth noting is that, in May 2001, judges started wearing black robes in courtrooms for the first time. In the middle of the robe there is a red stripe with four yellow buttons. This red is the colour of the national flag; the four yellow buttons are symbolic of the four layers of courts in China. Judges usually wear robes when they are in courtrooms. At the same time, a new business-like suit was introduced, which replaced the old one introduced in 1984 with its epaulette and caps that reflected its military origin. Judges now wear business-like black suits or light blue shirts at work. The change of the uniform and robe marked a change in the perception of the judiciary. The judicial profession is now recognized as differing from that of other civil servants.

Third, the Supreme People's Court has taken a leading role in promoting and strengthening judicial independence. The most remarkable manifestation is the release of the Code of Conduct for the Judiciary in 2001 (hereafter the Code), which makes China one of the few countries in the world with a specific code of conduct for the judiciary. The Code contains 50 articles, divided under the headings of six essential principles, namely: judicial impartiality, judicial efficiency, integrity of judges, judicial courtesy, self-improvement of judges, and restriction of extra-judicial activities. These general principles are similar to those provided in the U.S. Code.[21] However, the detailed rules within each principle also reflect Chinese characteristics.[22]

The Code's most relevant provisions concerning judicial independence include Article 2, which requires judges to uphold the principle of independence in carrying out their functions; they are not subject to interference by administrative organs, social organs or individuals. Article 11 stipulates that judges should be neutral in their handling of cases. Article 13 emphasizes that a judge should respect other judges right to adjudicate cases independently by not commenting on pending cases in the hands of others, not questioning or interfering in cases handled by lower courts and not requiring relevant information on cases handled by other judges. These are similar to the standards of internal independence of the judiciary as declared in the International Bar Association Minimum Standards of Judicial Independence (Standard 46).[23]

A fourth point to mention is that independence from external intervention has emerged in judicial practice. The most remarkable example is the recent so-called 'seed case'. It concerns a contract dispute between two companies handled by the Intermediate People's Court in Luoyang City, Henan province in 2003. The plaintiff insisted that compensation

---

21 For the text of the updated Code of Conduct for United States Judges, which became effective on 1 July 2009, see <www.uscourts.gov/RulesAndPolicies/CodesOfConduct/CodeConductUnitedStatesJudges.aspx>. Last visited September 2012.

22 Yuwen Li, 'Professional Ethics of Chinese Judges: a Rising Issue in the Landscape of Judicial Practice', (2003) 47 *China Perspectives*, pp. 28-39.

23 The IBA Minimum Standards of Judicial Independence. See <www.ibanet.org/About_the_IBA/IBA_resolutions.aspx>. Last visited September 2012.

should be decided according to the Seed Law of the People's Republic of China, whereas the defendant contested that the legal source should be the local Regulation on Seed issued by the People's Congress in Henan province. The trial judge, Li Huijuan, made the decision that the judgment should be based on the national law, and moreover she wrote in the judgment: 'After the national Seed Law became effective, the price of maize should be regulated by the market. The Regulation on Seed issued by the People's Congress in Henan province as local regulation which has lower status than the national law, and which is contradictory to the Seed Law, is invalid.'[24] The People's Congress Standing Committee in Luoyang City reported the judgment to the People's Congress Standing Committee in Henan Province and the latter issued a document indicating that the local Regulation on Seed was not contradictory to the national Seed Law, and that therefore the Judgment of the Court, which declared the invalidation of the local regulation, was an illegal review of the local regulation, violated the people's congress system and infringed upon the power of the People's Congress, and was thus a serious illegal act. Additionally, it requested the People's Congress in Luoyang City 'to exercise its supervisory powers according to law, correct the illegal act of the Intermediate People's Court in Luoyang City, and punish the persons involved in handling the case in the Court'.[25] Initially, Judge Li Huijuan was punished by the local court. However, as a result of media pressure and support from the Supreme People's Court, she was later cleared. Quite remarkably, the Supreme People's Court, in its 'Reply to the Request concerning the Contract Dispute Case of the Seed Company in Luoyang County and the Seed Company in Yichuang County in Henan Province', stated that a judge has the right to choose which law should be applied in deciding a case.[26] The gesture of the SPC was enthusiastically welcomed by academia both inside and outside of China. The prominent Chinese law expert of French origin, Stephanie Balme, compared Judge Li to the famous French Judge Magnaud.[27]

24 Liu Haibo, 'Cong Liangge Shijian Kan Woguo Zhongyang yu Difang Guanxi Tizhi' (From Two Events to Examine the System between Central and Local Relationship), in Li Lin *et al* (eds.), 'Yifa Zhiguo – Shinian Huigu yu Zhanwang' (Ruling the Country in Accordance with Law – A Decade of Retrospect and Prospect), (Beijing: Zhongguo Fazhi Chubanshe, 2007), pp. 415-418.

25 *Ibid.*

26 The Reply was issued by the SPC on 30 March 2004.

27 Stephanie Balme, 'Ordinary Justice and Popular Constitutionalism in China', in Stephanie Balme and Michael W. Dowdle (eds.), *supra* note 4, p. 180.

It should be noted that the topic of judicial independence received different attention under Xiao Yang, the former President of the SPC from 1998 to 2008, than it has under Wang Shengjun, the current President of the SPC. Xiao Yang emphasized judicial independence on many occasions. In 2007, he highlighted the four foremost tasks of deepening judicial reform in China, which are all relevant to judicial independence. First, he noted the task of prioritizing the disposition of judicial power towards a better arrangement of the functions of the internal organs of courts. This requires optimizing the division between trial organs and administrative organs; improving the relations between different levels of courts; and scientifically distinguishing the functions between higher and lower courts in order to establish a rational, reasonable clear division in the judicial structure. Secondly, he noted the task of strengthening and guaranteeing institutional capacity in carrying out adjudicative power independently and impartially in order to achieve greater judicial fairness. Moreover, he noted the need to continue to explore the reform of jurisdiction of administrative litigation in order to prevent any interference from local protectionism. Thirdly, he noted the task of improving the supervision system needed to ban requests for instruction by lower courts to higher courts concerning decisions on guilt, facts and evidence of a case in order to guarantee the independence of lower court and the supervisory function of the appellate court; establish a unified efficiency assessment system of adjudication quality; and establish and improve the disciplinary system for judges. Lastly, he noted the importance of the task of fostering a judicial force with high moral ethics and standardizing judicial conduct.[28]

In contrast, President Wang Shengjun emphasized judicial populism and judicial democratization. In an interview in 2009, he pointed out that in China courts are called people's courts. Thus, the nature of people's courts is to serve the people and the central task of courts in adjudication and enforcement of judgments is to solve the problems that are directly relevant to the people. In his view, judicial independence should not be emphasized one-sidedly in the process of judicial reform and that judicial reform in China should start from strengthening the weak aspects of the current judicial system and not just in transplant-

28 'Xiao Yang Tichu Sifa Gaige Sida Zhongdian: Jiaqiang Baozhang Sifa Duli' (Xiao Yang proposes four major tasks of judicial reform: the guarantee of judicial independence should be strengthened), available at <http://zqb.cyol.com/content/2007-11/24/content_1968901.htm>. Last visited September 2012.

ing a foreign system.[29] The impact of the shift of opinions on judicial independence as demonstrated by the two Presidents is that, in today's China, judicial independence is mentioned far less.

4.2 Characteristics of Judicial Dependence in Contemporary China

Recognizing the notable progress achieved over the past decades in China relevant to strengthening judicial independence, it is also useful to delve into elements that remain a destructive force against exercising judicial independence. These elements can demonstrate the dependence instead of independence of the judiciary. The ultimate goal of realizing fully-fledged judicial independence is to better serve judicial fairness in a harmonious society, which is desirable yet difficult to attain in many countries. I will examine the dependence factors from external and internal angles. The external elements include any interference with courts' work from various sources. Such interference mainly reflects, but is not necessarily limited to, obvious obstruction of courts' handling of individual cases. The less visible hindrances should also be addressed for the sake of a comprehensive understanding of the *status quo* and seeking practical solutions. An examination of the more interior aspects will focus on: the special procedures for handling cases within the courts; the competence of judges as relevant to the degree of independence the public can conceivably place on them; and the judicial corruption that inevitably undermines judicial independence in today's China.

4.2.1 *Major External Interference with Judicial Work*

Courts v. the Government

Whilst comparing judicial independence in Western countries with established democracies to Central-Eastern Europe and post-Soviet States, Seibert-Fohr pointed out that: 'While countries in transition from authoritarianism to democracy have to cope with an overwhelming executive branch, the search for adequate mechanisms to protect the judiciary from undue influence continues in older democracies

29 'Huang Songyou An: Zhongjiwei Hai Zai Cha' (Commission for Discipline Inspection of the Central Committee of the CPC is still investigating into the case of Huang Songyou), in *Nanfang Dushibao* (*Southern Metropolis Daily*), 12 March 2009. Available at <http://epaper.oeeee.com/A/html/2009-03/12/content_727638.htm>. Last visited September 2012.

too.'[30] Similarly, the tension between courts and the government cannot be overlooked when judicial independence in China is assessed.

A general perception in China is that courts are inferior to the government. A local court's finance is largely dependent on the local government. A renowned Chinese legal scholar once wrote that the courts' financial dependence on the government 'has put courts indirectly in a subordinate situation. They have to "look up the faces" of the administration'.[31] And 'those who manage the money bags manage those who manage the law'.[32] The achievement of local government is largely evaluated by the success of the local economy, and the local economy mainly relies upon local companies. All these are linked into a chain of interests and dependencies, which indefensibly results in local judicial protectionism. Local judicial protectionism is reflected in various facets of the judiciary.[33] The Supreme People's Court recognised that 'the emergence and extension of local judicial protectionism has seriously threatened the integrity and authority of our country's socialist legal system'.[34]

Another serious concern over courts' dependence on local government relates to administrative litigation. In 1989, the first Administrative Litigation Law (ALL) was enacted in China which authorizes courts to adjudicate cases brought by citizens or companies against specific acts of government agencies violating personal or property rights of citizens or legal persons. Nowadays, Chinese courts conclude approximately 100,000 administrative cases annually. Michael Palm observed that with 'the extensive nature and powers of bureaucracy in China, and the

30 Anja Seibert-Fohr, 'Conclusion: Judicial Independence in Transition', in Anja Seibert-Fohr (ed.), *Judicial Independence in Transition*, (Heidelberg: Springer, 2012), p. 1302.

31 Xin Chunying, *Chinese Courts History and Transition*, (Beijing: Law Press, 2004), p. 104.

32 Chris X. Lin, 'A Quiet Revolution: An Overview of China's Judicial Reform', (2003) 4 (2) *Asian-Pacific Law & Policy Journal*, p. 295.

33 Cai Dingjian summarized local judicial protectionism in six aspects: (1) some courts compete for jurisdiction by handling cases they should not in order to gain advantages in cases involving property or profit; (2) some courts refuse to file cases or postpone the hearing of cases so as to assist local parties; (3) some courts wilfully treat economic crimes as economic disputes so as to protect a local party's illegal gains; (4) some courts inappropriately apply coercive measures so as to be the first to control assets; (5) some courts misinterpret the law, distort the facts, and make unfair judgments in favour of the local party; (6) some courts make it difficult for non-local judgments to be enforced. See Cai Dingjian, 'Development of the Chinese Legal System since 1979 and Its Current Crisis and Transformation', (1999) 11(2) *Cultural Dynamics*, pp. 149-151.

34 See Research Department of the Supreme People's Court, *Renmin Fayuan Wunian Gaige Gangyao* (1999-2003) (Five-year Program for the Reform of the System of People's Courts 1999-2003), (Beijing: Renmin Fayuan Chubanshe, 2000).

growing rights-consciousness of the Chinese citizenry, it is surprising that the rate of increase of administrative suits has remained low'.[35] The work of Chinese scholars reveals that administrative litigation in China faces three main difficulties: having a case accepted by courts; having the case handled fairly; and enforcing a judgment in cases where the plaintiff wins. Courts' refusal to decide on administrative cases is a widespread complaint amongst Chinese lawyers. Where cases are accepted, courts in general are reluctant to deliver a judgment even when evidence can prove that the action of a governmental agency is illegal. Instead, courts try to reconcile the dispute between the parties involved by aiming to reach a reconciliation agreement rather than the courts having to deliver a judgment even though the Administrative Litigation Law clearly prohibits mediation in the handling of administrative disputes.[36]

Another notable phenomenon is that administrative chambers of courts have handled many more cases of executing administrative decisions brought by governmental agencies to courts than settled administrative cases brought by individuals or business entities against illegal or arbitrary administrative actions. The Figure[37] below illustrates that the number of administrative non-litigious execution are many more than the number of administrative litigation cases concluded by courts. One can surmise that judicial independence is critically significant when the government is a party to a dispute. It is absolutely indispensable that courts and judges are unbiased in favour of the government.

35 Michael Palm, 'Controlling the State: Mediation in Administrative Litigation in the People's Republic of China', (2006) 16 *Transnational Law & Contemporary Problems*, p. 179.

36 Jiang Bixin, *et al* (eds.), *Zhongguo Xingzheng Susong Zhidu De Wanshan: Xingzheng Susongfa Xiugai Wenti Shiwu Yanjiu* (Improvement of Administrative Litigation System in China: Practical Research on Revision of the Administrative Litigation Law), (Beijing: Falu Chubanshe, 2005).

37 The Figure is cited from He Haibo, 'Kundun de Xingzheng Susong' (Administrative Litigation in Dilemma), (2012) 2 *Huadong Zhengfa Daxue Xuebao* (Journal of East China University of Political Science and Law), p. 95.

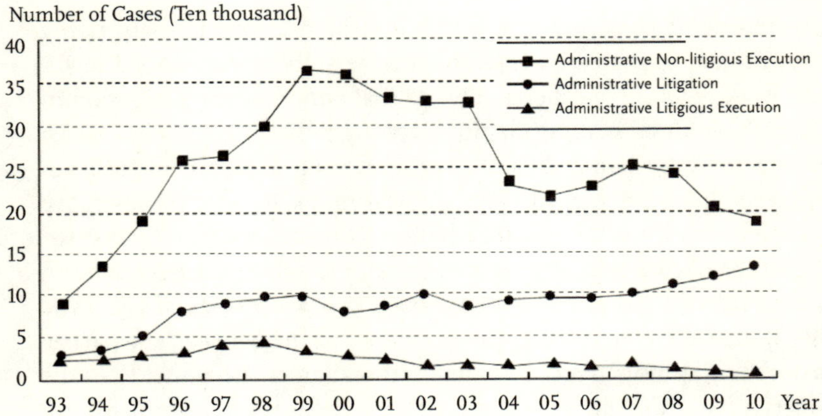

Courts v. the People's Congress

The relationship of the courts with the People's Congress as the highest power organ,[38] are mainly evident in two respects: People's Congresses appoint and dismiss presidents and judges of courts at the corresponding level;[39] and they supervise the implementation of law by courts. The routine supervision work takes place in various forms such as: the review and approval of the courts work report; review as to whether judicial interpretation is in compliance with the law; investigating and making proposals to courts on issues of serious public concerns; and handling petitions and complaints of alleged unlawful conduct by judicial officers.[40]

---

38 Art. 57 of 2004 Constitution of the People's Republic of China.

39 According to Arts. 62, 67 of the 2004 amended Constitution and Art. 34 of the 2006 amended Organic Law of the People's Court, the President of the Supreme People's Court is elected and removed by the National People's Congress, deputy presidents and judges of the SPC are nominated by the President of the SPC, and appointed and dismissed by the NPC Standing Committee. At the local level, presidents of local courts are elected and dismissed by the corresponding level people's congresses, deputy presidents and judges are nominated by the president, and appointed and dismissed by the people's congresses standing committees of the correspondent level. However, this is the procedure provided by the laws and can only be viewed merely as a formality since candidates have been first examined and approved by the relevant Party and government organs. China follows a system of 'Party controls the cadres'. Presidents of courts and judges are different ranking of cadres. The general rule is that the higher the position, the more political appointment it will be.

40 People's Congresses not only oversee judicial work, they provide oversight of the government as well. For the growing strength of local people's congress in overseeing the government, see Young Nam Cho, 'From "Rubber Stamps" to "Iron Stamps": The Emergence of Chinese Local People's Congresses as Supervisory Powerhouses', (2002) 171 *The China Quarterly*, pp. 724-740.

With regards to judicial independence, the most controversial issue is whether the supervisory power of a People's Congress can extend to interfering with individual cases handled by courts. This is the so-called system of supervision of individual cases by People's Congress. This system reached its most vigorous peak of influence in the 1990s, and has since diminished as a consequence of the enactment of the Supervisions Law in 2006. However, at local level, the system remains operational. In addition, in order to keep good relations with People's Congresses, some courts invite deputies to be people's assessors to sit on collegiate panels to decide cases alongside the judges.

Courts v. Media

Media coverage on judicial work is becoming more widespread in many countries, China is no exception. On one hand, the Party's control and censorship of media reports on judicial work continues to ensure that Party policy and instruction can reach the public through mass media. On the other hand, commercialization of media over the past two decades has rapidly strengthened media autonomy, resulting in more liberal media reporting of judicial work. Moreover, the internet revolution in recent years has opened new space for the public to promptly follow and even become engaged in the courts' handling of individual cases.[41]

As anticipated, media is playing a certain supervisory function over judicial work. A positive effect of such supervision is that some instances of outrageous injustice in criminal cases have been corrected in large part due to vigorous media reports.[42] This has also mobilised the reform of the criminal justice system with more emphasis being placed on the protection of the rights of the defendant and lawyer. At the same time, the emergence of investigative journalism and active use of web portals by legal scholars and lawyers to expose and discuss pending cases constitutes a new challenge to the judiciary. Courts are sometimes pressured to decide or alter judgments in response to a public outcry. This certainly causes instances of trial by media. The outcome of such influence can be a matter of life or death. A most recent high profile case that saved a life is the trial of Wu Ying. As a young business

41 For comprehensive academic research on media and court relationships in China, see Benjamin L. Liebman, 'The Media and the Courts: Towards Competitive Supervision?', (2011) 208 *The China Quarterly*, pp. 833-850. 'A Populist Threat to China's Courts?', in Margaret Y.K. Woo and Mary E. Gallagher (eds.), *Chinese Justice: Civil Dispute Resolution in Contemporary China*, (Cambridge: Cambridge University Press, 2011).

42 On the internet, if one types 'yuan an' (injustice case) in Chinese in Google search, one could find plenty of articles.

woman, she was convicted of financial fraud by a local court with the death penalty in 2009. She defended herself by claiming that she only borrowed money from friends and invested it in profitable businesses. The court of appeal sustained the original judgment. When the case was exposed, sensational public outcry was displayed in attacking the courts for punishing private business people too harshly while serious corrupted officials often receive lenient sentencing. On 21 May 2012, the Supreme People's Court overturned the local court's decision and charged her instead with a death penalty with a two-year reprieve.[43] The common practice in China is that if a convict does not commit new crimes whilst in prison during those two years, the death penalty can be reduced to life imprisonment or to a 20 to 15 year imprisonment.

In contrast, the similarly high profile case of Liu Yong has demonstrated another extreme result. Liu Yong, the head of a gang was sentenced by the Tieling Intermediate People's Court to the death penalty in 2002 for wilful bodily injury, deliberately damaging property, illegal business operations, bribery, gun possession and prohibiting law enforcement departments from carrying out their duties. Subsequently, Liu appealed, and in August 2003, the Higher People's Court in Liaoning Province charged Liu with the death penalty, with a two-year reprieve. The judgment of the Higher People's Court immediately caused wide public controversy. Articles and comments in newspapers, especially on the internet, swiftly attacked the decision of the Higher People's Court. Many people used aggressive words to describe Liu Yong as the enemy of the society. If he was not executed, who would be? The public attention and pressure led to the Supreme People's Court retrying the case directly. The SPC sentenced Liu to death for the crime of 'wilful bodily injury', Liu was executed immediately after being given the death penalty.[44]

Ideally, media and public views should not influence judges in making decisions in the application of law in individual cases. However, it may prove very difficult if judges are not responsive at all to public pleas. Fiss pointed out that: 'The power of judges is both limited and legitimated by the processes by which they exercise power – the need to listen to all the relevant parties and to justify their decisions in terms of

---

43 'Who goes to the gallows? Concern over a high-profile death penalty', <www.economist.com/node/21543593>. Last visited September 2012.

44 'Shenyang gang leader Liu Yong gets death penalty', <http://english.peopledaily.com.cn/200312/22/eng20031222_130952.shtml>. Last visited September 2012.

publicly acceptable reasons.'[45] In China, the situation can become more complicated when public views are politicised in the sense that they are used by the government to compel courts to judge cases by catering to popular view. This certainly undermines judicial independence.[46]

4.2.2 *Control of the Judiciary by the Communist Party*

The leading status of the Communist Party over the judiciary has several consequences. First, most judges are Party members. There is no publicly available statistic about the exact number of judges who are Party members. Based on some limited empirical work of Chinese scholars more than 70% and in some courts even 97% of judges are Party members.[47] A Party committee exists in each court to oversee the Party's ideology and disciplines to be followed by judges. The Party also provides regular training for judges at the Party's training institutes. As a member of the Party, judges are requested to adhere to the Party line on all Party-concerned issues. Most judges know deliberately or unintentionally how to reach decisions that will not contravene with or jeopardize the Party's policies.

In addition, the Party's control over the judiciary extends to the disposition of specific cases through its Political-Legal Committees. Such Committees exist at the central level down to the county level, with the main function of coordinating court, procuratorate and the police in handling complex and politically sensitive cases. At the local level, the members of such Committees consist of heads of court, procuratorate, police, department of judicial affairs, and often the secretary of the Political-Legal Committee who holds a concurrent post as head of the police. Where the court, procuratorate and police disagree, the Committee gives its opinion, and all will then follow. It is no exaggeration to conclude that this Committee 'is the most powerful actor in the criminal justice system ..., though it is not even mentioned in the

---

45 Owen Fiss, *supra* note 4, p. 59.

46 To a different degree such phenomenon can also occur in other countries. For instance, in analyzing judicial independence in the Netherlands Roel de Lange points out that 'the most pressing issue for judicial independence is political involvement in concrete criminal cases. There is notable pressure on the judiciary by way of public comments by members of parliament on sentencing practices, including attacks on the supposed partisanship of certain members of the courts'. Roel de Lange, 'Judicial Independence in the Netherlands', in Anja Seibert-Fohr (ed.), *supra* note 30, p. 271.

47 Si Weijiang, 'Zhongguo Sifa de Qianshi Jinsheng' (History and Present of Judiciary in China), available at <http://blog.caijing.com.cn/expert_article-151527-35996.shtml>. Last visited September 2012.

CPL [Criminal Procedure Law] or any related statute'.[48] Such practice inevitably prevents courts from independently handling cases and has caused some criticism in legal circles in China.[49]

4.2.3 Barriers to Judicial Independence within the Courts

The Relationship between Higher and Lower Courts

According to the Criminal Procedure Law, the Civil Procedure Law and the Administrative Litigation Law, an appellate court can remand a case to the first instance court for retrial if the facts in the original judgment are unclear or the evidence insufficient, or if the original court has violated procedural rules prescribed in the law. This is the so-called *Chongshen* (re-trial) system.[50] In practice, when a case is sent back, the court of appeal usually sends an internal document indicating which pieces of evidence are needed, which facts need to be clarified, what law should be applied and what the judgment should be. Although these could aid the lower court in deciding the case, it imposes opinions of the higher court on the lower court. Consequently, the latter can no longer make any independent judicial decisions.[51]

---

48 Sida Liu and Terence C. Halliday, 'Dancing Handcuffed in the Minefield: Survival Strategies of Defense Lawyers in China's Criminal Justice System', pp. 23-25, available at <http://papers.ssrn.com/sol3/papers.cfm?abstract_id=1269536>. Last visited September 2012.

49 Hou Meng, 'Sifa Gaige Beijing Xia De Zhengfa Zhili Fangshi: Jiceng Zhengfa Weiyuanhui Zhidu Ge'an Yanjou' (Governance of Political and Legal Affairs in the Background of Judicial Reform: Research on the Case of Local Political-Legal Committee), (2003) 5 *Huadong Zhengfa Daxue Xuebao* (Journal of East China University of Political Science and Law); Chen Youxi, 'Sifa Duli Shenpan Ying Cong Youhua Zhengfawei Rushou' (Modifying the Structure of Political-Legal Committee Should Be a Starting Point of Judicial Independence), *Nanfang Zhoumo* (Southern Weekend), 24 November 2011.

50 Art. 225 of the 2012 Criminal Procedure Law provides that: if the facts in the original judgment were unclear or the evidence insufficient, the court of second instance may rescind the original judgment and remand the case to the court that originally tried it for retrial; and remand of a case for retrial can only take place once. Art. 227 provides that, when a court of second instance discovers that the trial of the first instance court has violated litigation procedures, it can remand the case to the court that originally adjudicated it for a retrial. The violations include: (1) violations of the provisions of the Criminal Procedure Law regarding open trial; (2) violations of the withdrawal system; (3) deprivation of the parties litigation rights prescribed by law or restriction of such rights that may hamper impartiality of a trial; (4) illegal composition of a trial organization; and (5) other violations against the litigation procedures prescribed by law that may hamper impartiality of a trial. See also Art. 153 of the 2007 Civil Procedure Law. Art. 61 of the Administrative Litigation Law.

51 Chen Weidong and Li Fengfei, 'Xingshi Ershen "Fahui Chongshen" Zhidu Zhi Chonggou' (Redesigning the System of "Remand for Retrial" in the Second Instance Criminal Procedure), (2004) 1 *Faxue Yanjou* (Chinese Journal of Law), p. 124.

In addition, under the trial supervision procedures provided for in the criminal, civil and administrative procedure laws, there is a so-called re-trial system (*Zaishen* system).[52] It applies to a case if a definite error in a legally effective judgment is found. A president of court, a higher level court, the Supreme People's Court and the Supreme People's Procuratorate, or a party to the case can request a retrial of the case. The theoretical basis for the *Zaishen* system is the principle that 'wrong judgments must be corrected'. Some Chinese scholars argue that 'seeking truth was the ideological belief of the Party and should also guide courts in handling cases. If an effective judgment was wrong by error of either identification of facts or application of law, the judgment should be corrected according to the principle that wrong judgments must be corrected. It was unrealistic to expect that all judgments were correct due to the complexity of cases and limitations of judges. Some wrong judgments were unavoidable. If a case was wrongly judged, one must face the reality and correct it. In doing so, one could be called a good judge.'[53]

Lastly, there is also the system of request for instruction (*qingshi baogao zhidu*). This refers to the system whereby a lower level court asks a higher level court to give preliminary opinions on difficult or complicated cases and these opinions are taken as instructions and will be reflected in the lower court's judgment. Differing from the systems of remanding a case for re-trial and re-opening the trial of a case, the system of request for instruction is not provided for in any law. Instead, it has been developed as an informally improvised judicial practice. Liu Jachen, former Vice-President of the Supreme People' Court, once wrote: 'In most cases, when lower courts have difficult cases in hand, they request higher courts' opinions. The higher courts, if they have found that a case dealt with by lower courts may have greater impact, could take the initiative to give their instructions, this is conducive to correct the application of law and reduce the number of wrongly handled cases at the preliminary stage. This could reduce the litigation costs as a whole and facilitate litigation efficiency... if a higher court does not give timely instructions to a lower court, resulting in the

52 *Ibid.*

53 Chai Fabang (ed.), *Tizhi Gaige yu Wanshan Susong Zhidu* (Institutional Reform and Perfecting the Litigation System), (Beijing: Zhongguo Renmin Gongan Daxue Chubanshe, 1991), p. 273.

occurrence of wrongly-handled cases and causing harm to parties, this is considered as negligence of duty of the higher court.'[54]

The Adjudicative Committee

Each Chinese court has an adjudicative committee, which is the permanent highest adjudicative body consisting of the president, vice presidents, some heads of trial chambers and some senior judges. Apart from assembling judicial experience and other issues relating to the judicial work, the major function of such committees is to discuss and decide important or difficult cases. In judicial practice, when a collegiate panel handles an important or difficult case it should report its opinion to the head of the chamber. He in turn reports to the adjudicative committee. Then the committee discusses the case and makes a decision. This system leads to separation between the trial process and decision-making. Judges who are involved in the trial do not deliver the final judgement and members of the adjudicate committee who do not hear a case make the final decision for judges. This is the so-called 'handling a case in camera' (*anxiang caozuo*). Over the past two decades, the SPC has led local courts to reform the system of adjudicative committee by delegating more judgment-making power to individual judges and the collegiate bench. However, as a system, the adjudicative committee continues to exist in every court and decide many important and difficult cases.

Those who support the system have argued that it offers the possibility of using the collective wisdom of a court and of avoiding the limitations of a judge or a collegiate panel. They emphasize that most members of adjudicative committees are senior judges who have greater judicial and social experience. In contrast, Chinese judges are ordinarily younger and lacking in such experiences. Consequently, in their view, the adjudicative committee system can be used to reduce the incidence of misjudged cases. They also contend that, considering that judges can find themselves in a situation in which extra-judicial interference on cases is not uncommon and there is a lack of protection for individual

54 Liu Jachun, *Susong Jiqi Jiazhilun* (Litigation and Its Value), (Beijing: Beijing Shifan Daxue Chubanshe, 1993), pp. 46-47. Cited by He Weifang, 'Zhongguo Sifa Guanli Zhidu De Liangge Wenti' (Two Problems in China's Judicial Administration), (1997) 6 *Zhongguo Shehui Kexue* (China Social Sciences), p. 128.

judges against such interference, the adjudicative committee may use its collective power to deter external interference.[55]

4.2.4 *Judicial Competence and Its Relevance to Judicial Independence*

As I mentioned earlier, many judicial officers started their judicial career without formal legal education. Over the past three decades, the SPC has prioritised on-the-job training for most judges. The statistics show that the percentage of judges with university law degrees increased from 6.9% in 1995, to 51.6% in 2004.[56] However, it remains a fact that many judges, especially judges at the basic level courts, do not meet the academic qualifications for serving as a judge as required by the Judges Law. This certainly continues to affect overall judicial competence, and the level of judicial independence.

A more troublesome issue is the judicial corruption that consequentially dilutes judicial independence. Judicial corruption has expanded and intensified in parallel with the increasing role of the judiciary during the past two decades. In the early 1990s, the acceptance of dinner invitations and cash by judges gradually spread and became a 'hidden rule' for parties who aimed to achieve a favourable judgment. This individualized misconduct snowballed, and, nowadays, judicial corruption has escalated into an alarming degree of systemic and organized corruption within courts.[57] 'Ordinary citizens' perceptions of corruption in the judicial system narrowly range from total loss of faith in the nation's judges to believing that a significant portion of judicial officers are highly corrupt'.[58] According to the work report of the Supreme People's Court, approximately 401 judicial officials were punished for violation of law and discipline in 1988, ten years later the number increased

---

55 Chen Guangzhong and Daniel Prefontaine, (eds.), *Lianheguo Xingshi Sifa Zhunze Yu Zhongguo Xingshi Fazhi* (The United Nations Standards and China's Legal System of Criminal Justice), (Beijing: Falu Chubanshe, 1998), p. 93. See also Su Li, *Song Fa Xia Xiang* (Bring the Law to the Countryside), (Beijing: China University of Political Science and Law Press, 2000).

56 Zhu Jingwen (ed.), *Zhongguo Falu Fazhan Baogao, Shujuku he Zhibiao Tixi* (Report on China Law Development, Database and Indicators), (Beijing: Zhongguo Renmin Daxue Chubanshe, 2007), p. 34.

57 Zou Keyuan, 'Judicial Reform versus Judicial Corruption: Recent Developments in China', (2000) 11(3) *Criminal Law Forum*, pp. 323-351. Ting Gong, 'Dependent Judiciary and Unaccountable Judges: Judicial Corruption in Contemporary China', (2004) 4 (2). Judicial corruption is only one type of corruption. For corruption in China in general in terms of abuse of public power for private gains, see Ting Gong and Stephen K. Ma (eds.), *Preventing Corruption in Asia: Institutional Design and Policy Capacity*, (London: Routledge, 2009).

58 Liu Nanping, 'Trick or Treat: Legal Reasoning in the Shadow of Corruption in the People's Republic of China', (2008-2009) 34 *North Carolina Journal of International Law and Commercial Regulation*, p. 182.

to 2512.[59] Some Chinese scholars take the view that the actual figures are much higher than those officially reported.[60] Even so, one may argue that the number of judicial corruption cases is extremely small measured against the size of the judiciary. However, the collective harm it causes on public trust of the judicial system is huge. There is even a saying in China: the more judicial independence given to judges, the more judicial corruption one can expect. I for my part do not subscribe to such a view, I do however believe that the judiciary needs to be more accountable if they are expecting a greater degree of independence to be vested in them.

59 See the annual report of the Supreme People's Court to the National People's Congress in 1999 and 2009.

60 Li Ling, 'Corruption in China's Courts', in Randall Peerenboom (ed.), *supra* note 2, pp. 201-202.

5 Concluding Remarks: The Path to Achieving Effective Judicial Independence

Judicial independence as a general principle is recognized in the Chinese Constitution and other laws. Likewise, to a certain degree, judicial practice and reform over the past three decades have also improved and strengthened judicial independence. Nonetheless, to achieve a significant level of judicial independence in China, substantial progress is required in terms of both legislation and judicial practice. One can expect that substantive improvement on judicial independence cannot be achieved by one incident or in one 'big bang' in China. Rather, it is a complex process of advancing judicial quality, judicial systems, as well as political systems and social conditions that have effects on the functioning of the judiciary. Thus, I would venture to suggest advancing judicial independence by identifying a number of short-term goals and a long-term holistic systematic change.

The short-term goals can focus on two aspects. One is to improve judicial professionalism which constitutes a precondition for judicial independence. In observing the China situation, Keith Henderson indicated that it 'appears to be an opportunity to promote the personal independence of individual judges because many judges and scholars are receptive to adapting international best practices related to both substantive law and internal decision-making procedures to the evolving Chinese context. These reforms are generally seen as more realistic than more broad-based institutional and highly political reforms to achieve complete (or at least a high degree of) institutional independence.'[61]

Education and training for judges should cover legal knowledge, professional skills, as well as judicial ethics. In 2001, after the Code of Conduct for the Judiciary was issued, the Supreme People's Court organized nationwide training programs to foster judicial awareness on judicial impartiality, neutrality, independence and judicial professionalism. This has to a certain degree brought a fresh change, both to the minds of judges and to public images of judges and courts. However, in recent years the Supreme People's Court has shifted its focus

61 Keith Henderson, 'Halfway Home and a Long Way to Go: China's Rule of Law Evolution and the Global Road to Judicial Independence, Judicial Impartiality, and Judicial Integrity', in Randall Peerenboom (ed.), *supra* note 2, p. 29.

to emphasize that 'the judiciary serves the people', 'judicial populism', and 'judicial democratization'. Judges are required to be close to people, to mediate between disputants to reach agreements rather than to deliver judgments based on facts and according to law. In other words, the judicial character of a judge is weakened. This shift has generated confusion and criticism amongst judges and legal scholars in China and beyond. Some Western scholars call this 'China's turn against law'.[62] In the years to come, a new round of judicial reform can only be expected to turn the clock back.

The second dimension of the short-term goals can focus on changing those systems and habitual practices within courts in order to eliminate as many obstructions as possible to judicial independence. For instance, the system of requests for instruction by lower courts to higher courts should be abandoned to make courts more independent from one another. Without this system, the appeal procedure can serve effectively to correct wrong or improper judgments of lower courts. The system of the adjudicative committee should also be reformed in the manner that such committee's power to discuss and decide cases is maximally reduced. Decision-making power should vest with single judges or collegiate panels that conduct open trials. This is a judge's right as well as responsibility. In addition, some newly introduced systems which undermine judicial independence should be brought to an end. For instance, in recent years courts at all levels have initiated a system of inviting chief public prosecutors or deputy prosecutors to attend meetings of adjudicative committees. This obviously disrupts a court's independence from the procuratorate. When a case is discussed by the adjudicative committee, lawyers certainly do not have access to it, so neither should the procuratorate. For the essence of the independence of courts and judges is to decide a case within the court.

The long-term objectives entail substantial institutional change in law and practice. The relationship between the Party and the courts, and the other power organs and the courts, need to be adjusted to guarantee that judicial power can be independently executed without interference or restriction. Neutrality of judges should be fostered to a high level to prevent any political control over judges. The accomplishment of the long-term objectives can be comprehended more effectively in relation to the Chinese government's development strategy to strengthen the rule of law. Lubman once wrote: 'The rule of law is an ideology. Courts

62 Carl F. Minzner, 'China's Turn Against Law', (2011) 59 *Am. J. Comp. L.*, pp. 935-984.

truly dedicated to promoting that ideal cannot be instruments of a government that uses them to promote changing political tasks; they must have a more passive interest in solving conflict to attain a social equilibrium.'[63] The rule of law is the foundation as well as the guarantor for a long-standing economic prosperity and social stability. It cannot be accomplished without an independent and forceful judiciary.

From my lecture you can infer that to attain significant judicial independence in China is a challenging mission. However, this is not an impossible mission. In recent decades, China has come by leaps and bounds with fantastic economic achievements and the modernization of society, which demonstrates the country's capacity and the vigour to reform and progress. When I wrote this speech in the summer of 2012 in Beijing, the Olympic Games were taking place in London. I was utterly inspired by the miraculous achievement of Chinese athletes, who won a total of 88 medals which made China the second in the overall medal standings. I thought, and indeed remain of the belief, that with awareness and determination China can and must also achieve its goals of judicial reform, in which we strive for an independent and strong judiciary.

Now, at the end of this lecture I would like to express my wholehearted thanks to numerous people who have promoted me to the Chair of Chinese law. My gratitude to the Board of Directors of the Erasmus University Rotterdam and the Vereniging Trustfonds for the trust you lay in me. My particular thanks go to Professor Maarten Kroeze, the Dean of Erasmus School of Law. You have been extremely stimulating; the vision and confidence you give to me motivate my passion and professional dedication to the newly established Erasmus China Law Centre. A lot of appreciation also goes to Professor Ellen Hey, Professor Hans de Doelder, Professor Michael Faure, and Professor Edwin Bleichrodt, your support makes my professorship possible. I have fully enjoyed our cooperation in the past years and look forward to working with you in the years to come. My sincere thanks also go to many colleagues at the Erasmus School of Law. Though I am a new comer, your openness and friendly professional attitude enable me to join you, work efficiently and with pleasure.

63 Stanley B. Lubman, *Bird in a Cage: Legal Reform in China after Mao*, (Stanford: Stanford University Press, 1999), p. 297.

I owe a lot to Professor Cees Flinterman and Professor Jenny Goldschmidt. Your dedication to the discourse of international human rights has always been an inspiration for me. Looking back to my work experience at the Utrecht School of Law, one person who truly opened the door for my academic career in the Netherlands is Professor Fried van Hoof. In 1988, you offered me an AIO position and has since then guided me in completing my PhD thesis. What I learnt from you is now steering me in supervising other Chinese PhD candidates. My thanks to you is beyond expression. This also applies to my family in Beijing, particularly my parents, brothers and sister who are always with me despite the far distance. Talking about China, my mind cannot stop thinking and appreciating my teachers at the Law School of Peking University in the early 1980s, who had such a profound impact on my desire to learn and think law critically. They include in particular Professor Wang Tieya, Professor Zhang Guohua and Professor Li Zhimin.

Finally, a few words to my husband, Professor Nico Schrijver. Although you are always a bit embarrassed when I mention I was your student, in reality, you have always been my teacher (*laoshi* in Chinese). Your dedication to your work has transformed me into a bit of a workaholic as well. Your benevolence and generosity have influenced me over the years. I cannot conclude my appreciation of you in my life without mentioning our two lovely children: Lineke and Kees. Mama has seen you grow as I grow with you. I am so proud of you both for many reasons that I will not dwell on here, but one thing I must mention is your persistent support for mama to work. Here I am, standing before you; I trust you are happy for me.

Ik heb gezegd!